EXPLORING CAREERS IN
TV AND FILM

Acting in
TV and Film

Jeri Freedman

Cavendish
Square

New York

Published in 2019 by Cavendish Square Publishing, LLC
243 5th Avenue, Suite 136, New York, NY 10016

Library of Congress Cataloging-in-Publication Data
Names: Freedman, Jeri, author.
Title: Acting in TV and film / Jeri Freedman.
Other titles: Acting in television and film
Description: First edition. | New York : Cavendish Square, 2019. |
Series: Exploring careers in TV and film | Includes bibliographical references and index.
Identifiers: LCCN 2018018889 (print) | LCCN 2018021656 (ebook) |
ISBN 9781502640130 (ebook) | ISBN 9781502640123 (library bound) |
ISBN 9781502640116 (pbk)
Subjects: LCSH: Television acting--Juvenile literature. | Motion picture acting--Juvenile literature. | Television acting--Vocational guidance--Juvenile literature. | Motion picture acting--Vocational guidance--Juvenile literature.
Classification: LCC PN1992.8.A3 (ebook) | LCC PN1992.8.A3 F64 2019 (print) |
DDC 791.43028--dc23
LC record available at https://lccn.loc.gov/2018018889

Editorial Director: David McNamara
Editor: Kristen Susienka
Copy Editor: Rebecca Rohan
Associate Art Director: Alan Sliwinski
Designer: Christina Shults
Production Coordinator: Karol Szymczuk
Photo Research: J8 Media

The photographs in this book are used by permission and through the courtesy of: Cover Bob Jenkin/Alamy Stock Photo; p. 4 Kevin Fleming/ Corbis Documentary/Getty Images; p. 8 Entertainment Pictures/Alamy Stock Photo; p. 11 MoviePix/Getty Images; p. 12 Diane39/ iStock/Getty Images; p. 15 Hill Street Studios/Blend Images/Getty Images; p. 16 Siri Stafford/ Stone/Getty Images; p. 21 Lawrence K. Ho/Los Angeles Times/Getty Images; p. 23 Barbara Zanon/Getty Images; p. 26 Andrii Kobryn/Shutterstock.com; p. 28 Tasia Wells/WireImage/ Getty Images; p. 31 Sean De Burca/Shutterstock.com; p. 33 FilmMagic/Getty Images; p. 35 Zak Hussein/PA Images/Getty Images; p. 36 Anthony Devlin/PA Images/Getty Images; p. 37 Hulton Archive/Getty Images; p. 39 Gary Gershoff /WireImage/Getty Images; p. 41 Jasmin Merdan/ Moment/Getty Images; p. 44 ©Warner Bros./courtesy Everett Collection; p. 46 ©BBC One/ courtesy Everett Collection; p. 49 Jason Horowitz/The Image Bank/Getty Images; p. 52 Doug Menuez/Forrester Images/The Image Bank/Getty Images; p. 57 Roundex/Shutterstock.com; p. 61 Paul Bradbury/OJO Images/Getty Images; p. 66 ©New Line/courtesy Everett Collection; p. 69 Marc Piasecki/GC Images/Getty Images; p. 72 ©Warner Brothers/courtesy Everett Collection; p. 75 Earl Gibson III/Getty Images; p. 78 DFree/Shutterstock.com; p. 83 Monkey Business Images; p. 85 Angela Weiss/Getty Images.

Printed in the United States of America

CONTENTS

Actress Jess Walton performs on the set of the daytime drama *The Young and the Restless.*

CHAPTER ONE

The Actor's Life

In the twenty-first century, there are more opportunities than ever for actors in film and television because more films and TV series are being created than at any previous time. The United States is the third-largest film market by revenue, after China and India. In the United States, blockbuster movies costing hundreds of millions of dollars are usually made by large Hollywood studios, such as Disney, Time Warner (parent company of Warner Brothers), 21st Century Fox, Universal, and Viacom (parent company of Paramount). However, a much larger number—579 out of 718 films released in 2016, for example—are independent films, made with private financing as opposed to being paid for by a large studio. Their budgets are typically less than $20 million, in contrast to the typical large-studio budget of $100 million or more. Alternative media companies such as Netflix are also starting to engage in filmmaking. Some Hollywood studios have created divisions to fund and distribute independent movies. One example is Fox Searchlight Pictures, which has provided support for such films as *The Shape of Water*, which won the 2018 Academy Award for Best Picture.

Television is the medium with the largest viewing audience. The advent of streaming services such as Netflix, Amazon Video, and Hulu; networks such as CBS All Access, which shows content online; and on-demand services offered by cable and satellite TV providers have expanded the variety of the content available to viewers. Millennials, people born around the year 2000, are heavy users of mobile technology and are inclined to watch films and TV shows on devices such as smartphones and tablet computers. The ability to watch programming on more platforms has expanded the amount of time people spend watching shows. More consumption of programming means a greater demand for new shows and more jobs for actors.

Working as an Actor

In order to work as an actor in the film or television industry, an individual must join the film and television actors' union, the Screen Actors Guild–American Federation of Television and Radio Artists (SAG–AFTRA). At one time SAG and AFTRA were two separate unions, but they have merged, which means that membership in one automatically grants an actor the ability to work in both industries.

When a person is hired to act in a film, even as a background actor, or extra, he or she must join the union. To do so, the person presents proof of employment and pays an initiation fee. In television, actors have the opportunity to work in many types of shows, including series, miniseries, made-for-TV movies, talk shows, and reality shows. Working in any of these requires joining SAG-AFTRA.

The growth in companies producing television shows provides more opportunities than ever before for actors. Original television shows are being produced by broadcast television networks such as ABC, NBC, and CBS, as well as by cable networks like HBO and Showtime. Some of these networks are producing original content for their streaming TV services, such as *Star Trek: Discovery* on CBS All Access. Streaming video services, such as Netflix and Amazon Prime, are also producing original shows for online streaming. The need to constantly provide new content to binge-watching audiences has increased the opportunities for actors.

For those who are in high school and college, the delivery of videos over the internet by services such as YouTube has made it easy to create one's own videos or act in those being created by others. Such videos allow a person to display his or her skills and develop a following, providing an individual an excellent opportunity to hone his or her craft while still in school.

Types of Actors

Various types of actors participate in films and TV shows. Starring actors play the main characters of a story, and everyone wants to be a star. However, many actors have made successful careers out of playing supporting characters, the rest of the speaking parts in a film or TV show. Some actors who play supporting

Judy Garland was the star, or central character, of the film *The Wizard of Oz*.

roles go on to become stars. Others, especially those with a distinctive look, specialize in playing particular "types" for their entire career. For example, actor Danny Trejo has made a successful career playing villains. Background actors, also called "extras," play nonspeaking roles. They are the people who are seen in the background of scenes, walking down streets or participating in crowd scenes. Many actors started their careers as background actors and progressed to supporting actor roles before gaining starring roles. If one lives in a city where films and television shows are frequently shot—such as New York, Boston, New Orleans, Las Vegas, or cities in California, among others—it is possible to apply for a role as an extra when a film shoot is taking place in that city. Doing so gives a person a chance to gain professional experience while going to school or working at another job. Voice actors provide voice-overs or dialogue for animated films or TV shows and commercials.

One way to start learning about acting is to watch movies—lots of movies—and not just any movies. The best films to watch are those that have been recognized for their quality, such as the movies on the American Film Institute's list of 100 Greatest Movies or those that have won Oscars. Film critique website Rotten Tomatoes does polls of moviegoers, so it is a good source to see which films are popular with the public. The key is not just to watch movies, but to analyze what makes the actors' performances effective, then practice those skills.

Succeeding as an Actor

Many attributes help a person succeed as an actor. These qualities fall into two categories: technical and personal. Practical skills can be learned, and no matter how talented someone is, there are particular skills that he or she must acquire. Actors must be able to memorize large amounts of dialogue, but this is only the start of the skills an actor needs. Actors must have a knowledge of the practical techniques used to portray a character convincingly. They must be able to use their voice, body language, and gestures to express what a character is thinking and feeling. In addition to general acting skills, actors must learn different accents, how to perform pieces from different historical periods, and comedic as well as dramatic techniques.

Two other skills that are highly valuable to actors are singing and dancing, and it is common for aspiring actors to take lessons in these subjects.

A whole variety of practical abilities can benefit actors and extend the range of parts they can play. Among these are gymnastics for doing basic stunts, fencing, martial and other combat arts for use in fight scenes, skiing, motorcycling, horse riding, shooting, and the ability to play musical instruments, especially guitar and piano. Actors also need to be physically fit. This does not mean that they need to be slender—it means they need to exercise regularly so they can engage in physical activity without becoming short of breath, growing exhausted, or injuring themselves. They will be called on to engage in physical activity in the course of filming, such as running from someone, fighting, or dancing. They will have to work for long hours on set. Being physically fit means actors can better withstand the rigors of filming or taping.

Today, people can start to learn the required technical skills while in high school. In most cases, students will go on to study acting after high school in college, at schools specializing in dramatic arts or in private lessons and actors' workshops.

There have been instances when a person who was just right for a role was discovered and started his or her career in a starring role. However, such experiences are rare. Most actors start as background actors or in small parts. Given this, it is important to impress others involved in the production with the fact that one is pleasant and cooperative to work with. Actors might have to deal with a director and other professionals who are stressed and under pressure.

Fencing is an example of a technical skill, used often in historical films. Here, actor Yul Brynner practices with a fencing coach on a set in 1958.

Actors have to work long hours, and when starting out, they may have to spend a long time just waiting until they are needed. They must be able to deal with frustration, weariness, and boredom without becoming irritable. As they become recognizable to the public, they will have to deal with the intrusion of members of the public and the media into their personal life. They must be able to remain calm, deal politely with fans, and control their temper when questioned by members of the media.

Actors must be problem solvers. They have to break down their own part and figure out how to

An actor analyzes a script, deciding how to portray his character.

best portray what their character is thinking and feeling in each shot. They have to adjust to difficult working conditions on location and work around problems they encounter on set. They must be flexible—able to improvise, adjust to changes in the script or environment, adapt to schedule changes, and juggle multiple demands on their time. They are also expected to pitch in as needed to help promote a project.

Actors must pay attention to their diet and sleep. Often actors have to be on set in the wee hours of the morning and work until late at night. Eating well, exercising, and getting as much sleep as possible are important to remaining healthy.

Actors require strong listening skills so that they are able to interpret what the director wants from them in a scene. Good listening skills are also important to remaining safe when doing stunts or participating in action scenes. Actors must have good organizational skills so they can deal with the demands of daily life and commitments, as well as those of work. They must be able to establish priorities, arrange tasks in an order that will allow the most important ones to be accomplished first, and manage their time efficiently.

The core of acting is being creative. Actors must use their imagination and develop original ideas. They must be willing to expose their emotions to the audience. The ability of an actor to portray a character is highly related to his or her knowledge of people. Actors need to understand not just the superficial aspects of human behavior, such as the way people speak or how they look, but also the little details that affect the way that different types of people behave with others such as peers, bosses, and enemies. Actors need very good observational skills to study people in real life and learn the details that can make a performance convincing and moving. They must pour themselves into their part with energy and passion, which can be the difference between an OK actor and a great one.

Actors must have an understanding of and insight into human psychology. To portray human behavior, they must understand people's motivations, thought processes, and emotional responses. It's possible to gain insight into human psychology by reading books on the subject, but an actor also needs to observe firsthand how psychological forces affect people's behavior. Actors must constantly study people and analyze the reasons for their behavior and the things they say. All of this will contribute to their ability to create characters.

To succeed as an actor, a person has to be willing to work hard, not just on set but also when looking for work. When he or she is starting out, it is necessary to be rigorous about researching upcoming projects and auditioning for parts. Even successful actors stay in contact with producers and directors, as well as their agents, to find new projects. It also takes confidence to be an actor. Often great persistence is required to keeping pursuing an acting career, so the person needs to believe in himself or herself. Confidence is also a must for people who will have to expose themselves onscreen. Actors who are willing to be vulnerable— even when doing so exposes them to criticism—often give the most outstanding performances. That said,

Rehearsing their lines allows actors to arrive at the most effective delivery.

not every member of the public or media critic will like the actor's performance. In any creative profession, a person must be able to take criticism as well as praise. Being an actor is not easy, but it can be highly rewarding, creative, and ultimately successful.

An actor on set works with a team of cast and crew members.

CHAPTER TWO

Working with a Team

Creating a film or TV show requires a large group of professionals, including executive, creative, production, and support personnel. Because of the collaborative nature of filmmaking, it is important for actors to work in a professional manner with all members of the team, even when conditions are uncomfortable or stressful. The relationships between members of the team can determine whether or not a film or show succeeds.

Senior Creative Professionals

The producer and director of a film or TV show and their staffs are responsible for the overall production. They hire the heads of key departments and have the final say on financial and artistic decisions. The producer finds or approves an original script, a book or work from another medium to be adapted, or a concept for a series. He or she then obtains funds to finance the project. This might mean getting approval from the senior management at a film studio or TV network to go ahead with the project, or lining up private individuals or companies to provide funding.

Once funding is achieved, the producer creates a budget. During filming or taping, he or she must either make sure the film stays within the budget or obtain additional financing. The producer usually also hires the director and writers for a project. The producer's staff includes the line producer, who tracks expenses and manages the budget; one or more associate producers, who assist the producer; a production assistant, who performs support tasks for the producer and his or her team; a production coordinator, who handles logistics, such as renting equipment and making sure that people and resources are where they need to be when they are needed; and a production secretary, who handles scheduling, invoicing, and paperwork.

A movie director has artistic control over a film. He or she chooses the heads of the production teams and actors, and makes the final decision regarding the creative design of the project, including sets, costumes, hair, makeup, special effects, and music. He or she also has the final say in how the movie is filmed. Once filming is completed, the director works with the film editor to create the final version. One or more assistant directors reports to the director. They help him or her as required, performing tasks such as managing the shooting schedule, ensuring the crew is in place, and arranging the background actors. The casting director is responsible for arranging auditions or interviews for actors. He or she works closely with the producer and director to provide actors who are appropriate.

In television, the director's role varies according to the type of show being shot. When making dramas, miniseries, and made-for-TV movies, the director's role is similar to that of the film director. The major limitation is that the director of an episode must maintain the nature of the characters and the set established for an ongoing series.

Sitcoms are usually shot with multiple cameras while the actors perform continuously, as if they are on a stage. In this case, the director's role is primarily to rehearse the actors and provide their blocking (movement) prior to filming. After shooting several takes, or versions, of each scene, the director, the producer, and editor choose the best takes to appear in the final version on TV.

The screenwriter crafts the script. He or she creates the sequence of events that occur in the film or TV show, defines the characters, and writes the dialogue for the actors. The cinematographer, or director of photography (DP or DOP), shoots or supervises the shooting of the film. The cinematographer and director work together to design the camera angles and shots that will give the final production its unique look and feel. On large productions, the camera is run by the camera operator rather than by the cinematographer. On small productions, the cinematographer will operate the camera with the help of an assistant cinematographer. The lighting for shots is handled by a gaffer. He or she indicates where lights are to be placed and puts filters on lights to change the color of the light or its nature, making the light softer or more intense. Sound mixers record the audio generated during the filming process, including the dialogue. They place microphones on each actor and record their dialogue separately. That way, the sound mixer can adjust the audio level from each microphone individually.

The Production Crew

The head of the production team is the production manager, who oversees the administrative aspects of the production departments. Production managers do not make creative decisions; they manage the production budget and approve expenditures. They also arrange for equipment, subcontractors, and locations for shooting. The production designer/art director is responsible for the "look" of a film or TV show. He or she works with the set, costume, makeup, hair, and prop department heads to ensure a consistent tone that meets the director's expectations. On small productions, the production designer is also the art director. In large projects, the production designer has a second-in-command, who is designated as art director. In this case, the art director interfaces with the production department heads to ensure that their designs match the concepts of the production designer, and that work stays on schedule. The prop master acquires, inventories, and manages the props used on the production. A prop is any movable piece of set decoration—for example, weapons, telephones, and dishes.

The artists in three departments work directly on actors: costume, makeup, and hair. The costume

Costume designer Soyon An displays the wardrobe she's created for the TV show *American Idol*.

designer creates the concepts for the clothing worn by the actors. He or she selects the fabrics, colors, and accessories to be worn by the actors, and the wardrobe stylist prepares the actors' clothing and accessories. Wardrobe assistants clean and maintain the clothing and accessories, help distribute the wardrobe, and return items to inventory. Dressers assist the actors with their clothing changes.

The key makeup artist, or makeup designer, creates the concept for the makeup that will be used in each shot. Makeup artists apply the makeup and any prostheses required to change the shape of an actor's face or head. Special-effects makeup artists create prostheses and apply makeup to radically change an actor's face and head, as well as create wounds and scars. The key hairdresser or hair designer creates the concepts for the hairdos of the actors. Hairdressers cut, style, and color actors' hair. Both makeup artists and hairdressers have assistants who perform basic tasks and help as necessary.

The stunt coordinator arranges the sequences in which stunts are performed by a stuntman or stuntwoman. Actors who perform their own stunts will also work with the stunt coordinator. The special effects coordinator designs the special effects and oversees their creation. Special effects technicians use mechanical and electronic means to make the special effects, which include fires, explosions, weather, and objects that break, shatter, or collapse. Actors might be present on set while these special effects are in action. Visual special effects (VFX) are created on computers. They are designed by the VFX coordinator and created by VFX technicians.

A stuntman, standing in for actor Johnny Depp, performs a stunt where he jumps from a balcony.

Working with the Team

Actors sometimes see themselves as the center of the movie or TV universe because their performance is central to the success of the film. But how they behave and interact with each other, and with members of the production crew, also has a great impact on the working environment and the success of the production. Actors must trust other members of the cast and the production staff with whom they interact, such as makeup artists, hair stylists, and wardrobe staff. The cast needs to set the tone for the production

THE PERKS OF AN ACTING CAREER

There are many perks to being an actor. Acting is rarely boring. Actors face the challenge of creating characters from different walks of life, and sometimes different time periods. They may even find themselves playing otherworldly characters. They get to work on different types of projects and with a variety of people. Acting is creative. Actors may get to experiment with approaches and genres. Giving a successful performance is immensely gratifying, and receiving recognition from critics and fans is even more satisfying.

Film and television projects provide the chance to develop friendships with other actors, producers, and directors. If an actor gets along well with the others involved in a project, this can lead to other opportunities. Actors can gain recognition from the public and possibly win awards. They also have the opportunity to travel and experience different cultures.

A person can be an actor at any age—child, teen, adult, or older person. Actors can choose when they want to work. It's not just stars who have the luxury of working only when they wish. Many people who work as background actors do so to supplement their income from other jobs. True, if a person is in a highly demanding managerial position, it's unlikely that he or she also has time to be an actor. However, college students with the summer free, people employed on a part-time or freelance basis, and those who have flexible work hours or are retired can apply for parts as background actors when films or TV shows are being shot in the area. Often actors with a variety of ages, physical appearances, and ethnicities are needed for background roles, and a diverse group of actors is hired.

As a person gains recognition as an actor, he or she can make significant money and select projects of particular interest to work on. If actors make a lot of money, they have the ability to use some of it to support causes they believe in.

A skilled makeup artist can significantly enhance an actress's appearance.

by behaving in a professional manner and treating everyone with courtesy, even when disagreements arise. Because time for dressing, makeup, and hair is often limited by the shooting schedule, it is important to be professional and arrive on time.

When dealing with the creative aspects of a production, actors need to be willing to discuss approaches they think might enhance a performance, or ones that they feel are not working. At the same time, they have to realize that they might have to compromise for the benefit of the overall finished work. Once a decision has been made, they must be willing to do their best to follow it. Indeed, they must always be willing to do their best, no matter how big or small a project. The quality of an actor's performance can make or break a production.

Actors must have their lines learned when shooting begins. Some TV shows are shot with the actors reading their lines from a teleprompter atop the camera, but even so, they should be familiar with what they are to say. Before shooting starts, an actor must adequately rehearse his or her portrayal of the character so that the performance is natural and effective. Actors must take the time to understand their characters so that they can provide the little details that will make the role believable.

Actors need to be flexible and willing to audition, rehearse, get prepped, and work when needed, and they must be able to adapt to working on location, sometimes in uncomfortable circumstances. They must be able to take practical problems in stride, as well as changes to the production's concept and script.

Professionalism means a person keeping his or her temper and being patient even when the person has to spend long hours standing around until needed, sit in a makeup chair for hours while special effects makeup is applied, or shoot at the end of a long day. Actors should be willing to support other actors and members of the production team. They need to be able to give constructive advice or suggestions without offending other team members or criticizing them. Actors are the central figures in the production, and if they maintain a positive attitude, this will go a long way toward making the set a pleasant place to work. Creating a sense of camaraderie among team members improves collaboration and results in a higher-quality product. For actors starting out, a pleasant, positive attitude is particularly important. It leads more established actors to like them and makes the producer and director want to work with them again.

In the costume department, actress Gabrielle Walsh (*right*) is dressed for her performance by a fashion stylist.

CHAPTER THREE

The Actor at Work

Film and television production takes place in three phases: preproduction, production, and postproduction. The preproduction phase consists of all the activities that occur before shooting starts. The production phase covers the actual shooting, or "principal filming." The postproduction phase includes all the activities that take place after shooting is complete, to create the final version of the project.

Before Production Starts

The preproduction period for films and TV series can last weeks to months. When a pilot episode, or very first episode, of a TV series is made by an independent studio to sell a series to a network, the entire preproduction period might have to begin all over again when the series is purchased, if the network wants significant changes or a different cast.

Before actors can prepare for filming a production, they have to get hired. Big stars might be invited by a producer or director to participate in a project. They might even have a script written specifically for them. In most cases, however, actors have to audition to win a part in a movie or TV show. At the audition, actors perform a scene from the script while being filmed or videotaped.

The audition process begins with the casting director receiving a copy of the script and a list of the actors required, including their gender, age, and (if relevant) ethnicity. The casting director posts notices for a casting call in industry trade publications, such as *Variety* and the *Hollywood Reporter*, and on internet sites such as backstage.com. Both actors and agents, who represent actors, read these sources—known as "the trades"—to see what projects are being started that need actors. The actors or their agents then contact the casting director to arrange an audition. Often, casting directors give priority to actors they know or agents they trust. They will audition new actors either at an open casting call, at which anyone can try out, or after receiving a video from an aspiring actor who wishes to audition. The video gives the casting director the opportunity to see the unknown actor performing, and if he or she is impressed, the actor will be invited to audition. Willow Shields won the role of Primrose Everdeen in *The Hunger Games* by submitting a video of herself playing the role. At an audition, actors are taped reading for the role, then the director and producer study the videos. They either hire actors or have the casting director arrange a callback, if there is more than one actor they are considering for the part, so they can make a final decision.

To prepare for an audition, actors need to practice reading passages from scripts. The best approach is to practice regularly, videotaping themselves and then

An actor at an audition reads a scene featuring a character he wants to portray.

reviewing the video until they are satisfied with their performance. The audition might or might not win the actor the part, but it's not unusual for the same casting director to see that actor multiple times at auditions for different projects. Therefore, it's important to give the best performance possible. The actor might not be right for a particular film, but giving a good performance and being professional can create a good impression on the casting director, and influence his or her desire to hire the actor in the future.

To audition for TV shows, it's necessary to understand what is successful—or not—on TV. Therefore, aspiring TV actors need to watch lots of different sorts of TV shows. Becoming familiar with the different styles of acting in various TV shows makes it easier to give an appropriate performance, both in an audition and on the set. It is also beneficial to watch famous old TV shows. References to or catchphrases from old shows pop up in current ones ("Beam me up, Scotty" from the original *Star Trek*, for example). Directors often refer to characters in old shows to tell actors how they want them to behave ("Do it like you're Mulder in *The X-Files*"). When auditioning for a part in a series, it's important for an actor to watch half a dozen recent episodes so he or she can project a style that is appropriate for the series.

After being hired, an actor does a detailed reading of the script to prepare for the role and analyzes how the character thinks, feels, and responds in each scene. Actors must not only learn their lines but also review their part and lines every day to perfect their portrayal of the character. Some actors do research as part of the preparation process. This is particularly likely if the character is a historical or a living person, if the project is part of an ongoing series, or if the show is based on a property from another medium such as a book or series of books. Some actors, such as Daniel Day-Lewis, go as far as to try to act as if they are their characters as they go through their daily life, in the weeks leading up to filming. In some cases, an actor needs to learn a particular skill prior to the start of filming, such as using a weapon or playing a musical instrument.

Before the production starts, the director will rehearse the actors. If the film or TV show requires singing and dancing, the actors will also rehearse with the musical director and choreographer (the person who designs and directs dances). In preproduction, a

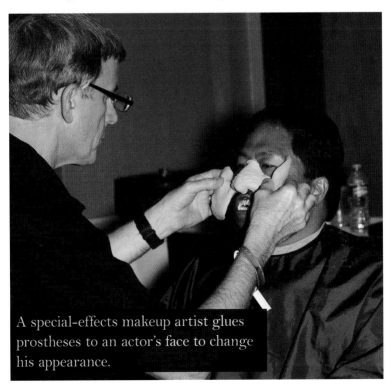

A special-effects makeup artist glues prostheses to an actor's face to change his appearance.

shooting schedule is drawn up, which lists the order in which scenes will be shot and the scheduled dates and times. Actors will have sessions with the makeup department. If someone needs a facial prosthesis or a mask, a special-effects makeup artist will make a cast of his or her face. In this case, the makeup artist will make a plaster mold of the actor's face to cast a replica to work from. If an actor needs to be fitted with false teeth (such as vampire fangs), contact lenses, or glasses, he or she will have sessions with a dentist or optician to get fitted.

Actors also need to be fitted for costumes. This might entail a number of fittings. If their hair needs to be dyed, they will have this done by the hair department. Actors might participate in preshoots, which are used to test the lighting, wardrobe, and makeup. The director uses the preshoots to ensure that the actors' hair, makeup, and costumes will create the effect he or she wants. Actors may also be asked to pose in costume and makeup for publicity material such as posters.

Production

The process of shooting a film is similar to shooting a television show, although films are often more elaborate in terms of length, number of shots, and variety of locations. When shooting starts, the actors begin their production routine. They arrive very early in the morning and go to the costume, makeup, and hair departments to be prepared. Then they report to the set. Scenes are often shot out of order so that all those in a certain location can be shot at the

In an on-location shoot, filming often takes place outdoors in a natural environment. Here, actor Danny Dyer is in London filming *The Rapture*.

same time, which minimizes time spent transporting actors and equipment from one place to another. Actors and crew are issued a schedule in advance that shows the scenes that will be shot each day. Prior to shooting a scene, it's usual to do a rehearsal. At that time, the director will have actors stop at certain physical locations, which are marked with small pieces of tape. The actors will stop on these "marks" during the shooting.

When the director is ready to shoot a scene, the actors in that scene take their starting positions. A person designated by the director steps in front of the camera and holds up a clapboard (a small square board with a hinged piece at the top) with the scene

THE LORD OF THE RINGS

SCENE	TAKE
RK371P	1

F.P.S.		ROLL #
2	32 mm	A2O2

A clapboard records the scene and take number of a shot and provides a sound to synchronize it with the soundtrack.

and take numbers written on it. The person calls out the scene and take number—for example, "Scene 12, take 1"—and snaps the hinged part down on the clapboard, which creates an audible "crack." The purpose of the clapboard is to allow the director and film editor to identify each version of every scene shot, when editing the film. The purpose of the sound is to help synchronize the sound recording with the visual recording, because sound is recorded separately from the visual portion.

The director calls "Action!" and the actors begin to perform. Sometimes partway through a scene, the director will call "Cut!" Then the camera is stopped, and the actors return to their starting positions. This might occur if there is a problem, such as an actor flubbing a line or a piece falling from a set. At other times, the director might want to make a change in the way a scene is being performed. Each scene might be shot multiple times before the director gets a version he or she is satisfied with. At that point, the director says "Cut. Print it!" and the scene is done.

Films and high-end television shows often use multiple cameras. This allows the director and cinematographer to capture images from different distances and angles. After the scene is shot, actors might be asked to do close-up shots, also called "reaction shots." This is a shot of the actor's face showing his or her reaction to what another actor is saying, or to something he or she sees. For example, a close-up of an actor might show her looking horrified

A reaction shot focuses attention on an actor's reaction to an event or situation and is used to emotionally affect the audience. Here, Christopher Walken's character reacts to events in the film *Sleepy Hollow.*

MERYL STREEP

Meryl Streep, who many critics consider to be the greatest contemporary actress, is an example of an actress who started performing while in high school. She was born Mary Louise Streep in 1949 in Summit, New Jersey. On SimplyStreep.com, Streep says of herself, "I was an ugly little kid with a big mouth, an obnoxious show-off." She got her first taste of show business at twelve in a school Christmas concert when she sang "O Holy Night" in French. Her singing was so impressive, her teachers encouraged her to pursue becoming an opera singer. According to biographer Michael Schulman, "She had scraggly short hair [and] cat-eye glasses that made her look like a middle-aged secretary." Then, she became interested in boys and decided she wanted to be beautiful and popular. She studied magazines like *Seventeen* and *Cosmopolitan* with much the same intensity that she would later apply to preparing for her film parts. She replaced the glasses with contact lenses, dyed her hair, and joined the cheerleading squad. She won the title of homecoming queen in her senior year.

It was in high school that Streep began acting in plays, starring in school productions of *Li'l Abner* and *Oklahoma*. Streep entered Vassar College in Poughkeepsie, New York, as a music major but realized that her passion was acting. She went on to get her master's degree from the renowned Yale Drama School in New Haven, Connecticut. Her first film role was

Meryl Streep has starred in such critically acclaimed films as *The French Lieutenant's Woman, Sophie's Choice, Julie and Julia,* and *Mamma Mia!*

Anne Marie in the 1977 movie *Julia.* The following year, she received her first Oscar nomination for her role as Linda in *The Deer Hunter.* Streep won Best Actress Academy Awards in 1980, 1983, and 2012 for her performances in *Kramer vs. Kramer, Sophie's Choice,* and *The Iron Lady,* respectively. She has received a total of twenty-one Oscar nominations.

after hearing frightening news, or tearful after her boyfriend says he's leaving her. Between scenes and before close-ups, makeup artists and hair stylists on set might touch up an actor's hair and makeup. It is up to these artists to make sure that hair and makeup not only look perfect but that they also look the same in the distance and close-up shots for the scenes. For example, if an actress has a curl of hair behind her ear in the long shot, it must be in the same place in the close-up.

When the shooting of one scene is completed, the next scene is called. Despite the fact that they started work early in the morning, actors might have to work late into the evening, shooting one scene after another. Therefore, it is important for actors to stay in shape, not just so that they look good on camera, but because performing can require a great deal of stamina.

After Shooting Stops

During postproduction, a film or TV show is edited. The film editor works with the director to choose and combine shots. The music director, sound editor, and sound mixer add music and sound effects, then adjust the sound levels on the soundtrack. The soundtrack is combined with the visual film or video. If digital special effects are part of the film, they are added at this time as well by visual effects artists, who create them using computer systems.

Actors are typically not involved in postproduction, with one exception—rerecording dialogue. Sometimes dialogue recorded during filming is not "clean" because there is extraneous noise, such as the ringing

A sound engineer reviews film footage and flags points where actors' dialogue needs to be rerecorded.

of a phone or a siren from a passing ambulance or police car. In this case, the sound editor flags the affected line(s) for rerecording in the studio. The problem of background noise is particularly prevalent when filming on location, rather than on a soundstage at the studio. The process of substituting new dialogue for that recorded on the soundtrack is called automated dialogue replacement (ADR).

When doing ADR, the actor watches the scene on a screen and reads his or her dialogue into a microphone, matching it to the movements of his or her mouth onscreen. For a movie, usually the lead actors are brought in first, one at a time. Each is given a copy of the script and shown the final version of the movie onscreen. At this point, the movie is complete with sound, but for the purpose of recording the voice-over, all the sounds are silenced. At the points where the dialogue needs to be redone, the actor speaks that dialogue into a microphone. Once the major actors are done with their dialogue, any necessary supporting actors repeat the same process. When all the dialogue voice-overs are done, the music and any other final audio touches are added to complete the project.

For a television show, the process is slightly different. Generally, after the shooting of a day's scenes is completed, the actors go to a recording room, where they again read the dialogue so that clean dialogue is ensured. The sound crew then adds any music, laugh tracks, and other sounds if required.

Voice-Over Actors

Voice-over actors specialize in voice acting—that is, performing dialogue for films, TV shows, or commercials, but not acting onscreen. Voice-overs are needed for several different purposes in film and television. They are used in live-action films in which one or more characters is computer-generated, such as in the film *Avatar*, or in which a character wears special-effects makeup or a costume that makes it impossible to record his or her voice during shooting (as was the case with Darth Vader in the original *Star Wars* trilogy). In that case, the character's dialogue is recorded separately as a voice-over.

Voice-overs are also used for the dialogue in animated television shows such as *The Simpsons* and animated films such as *Zootopia*, as well as for narration in documentary television shows such as *Mysteries at the Museum*, documentary films, and commercials. A related type of voice acting is "looping," in which voice actors are brought in to record background conversation to go with footage of background actors in specific scenes, such as the muttering of angry townspeople.

The process of dubbing, or replacing English dialogue in a film with a foreign language, is similar to recording ADRs. Because there are several major foreign markets for American films, major Hollywood movies are often dubbed into languages such as French, German, Spanish, and Chinese for foreign release. The process is expensive, since the entire dialogue must be rerecorded. Therefore, the process is usually only done for films produced by major film studios. Generally, animated films are dubbed into a greater number of languages than live-action ones. This approach is necessary because a large portion of their audience is children, some of whom can't read subtitles.

When a film is dubbed, the English dialogue is removed from the soundtrack, leaving the music and sound effects. An actor working with a translated copy of the dialogue speaks into a microphone while trying to match the movements of the actor's mouth onscreen. Usually the dubbing actor is different from the one who originally played the role, but in some cases, if the original actor speaks the language being dubbed in, he or she may do both versions of the film. This is different from the process used to make animated projects.

Animated Film and Television Shows

Animated films usually start with the actors recording the dialogue spoken by their characters, and the animation is added later. There are several reasons

Actor Zach Galifianakis records the dialogue for the Joker in *The LEGO Batman Movie.*

for this approach. First, it is extremely difficult for an actor to lip-sync dialogue to match the facial movements of an animated character, especially if the character is not a human being. Even if this could eventually be achieved, it would require an enormous number of takes, which would make the process much more expensive and time-consuming. More important than the physical limitation is the fact that even in an animated film, where the actor's body won't be seen onscreen, he or she is paid to act—to vocally portray a range of emotions and attitudes. To achieve an effective result, an actor's delivery of the dialogue depends on elements such as timing, pauses, intonation, and phrasing (drawing out certain letters or syllables of words). If an actor had to conform his or her reading to match prerecorded animation, this would most likely make the dialogue sound unnatural and limit the actor's ability to develop the character's personality.

At one time, actors who specialized in creating various voices for animated characters provided the dialogue for cartoons and animated films. This is still common in television. However, most big-budget animated films, such as those produced by Disney/Pixar and Dreamworks, use well-known actors to voice the characters. The practice has become so prevalent that many of the characters in animated features are drawn to incorporate features of the actors who are "playing" them. Indeed, audiences have come to expect animated characters to resemble the actor voicing them.

When an actor works on an animated film, the director provides information about the personality and nature of the character and works with the actor to achieve the desired effect. The actor reads the character's dialogue from the script, creating a unique vocal quality for the role. Often the actor records lines in several different ways so that the director can apply the version he or she deems most appropriate when the film is assembled.

After all the actors have completed recording their dialogue, digital graphic artists create the animation

A digital animation artist creates animation to be combined with the recorded dialogue.

to make it look as if the characters are speaking the dialogue. The film editor chooses the version of each actor's recorded lines that he or she thinks is most effective in a scene and combines them with the animation. Often, voice actors working on animated television series record more than one episode at a time.

Developing Acting Skills

There are two ways to develop acting skills while in school: classes and practice. Students who want to become actors often take classes in acting after school or over the summer. Such courses are offered by community colleges, local theaters, and private acting schools. However, if you are interested in being an actor, don't restrict yourself to acting classes. Taking classes in dancing and singing can make you more versatile and increase the range of roles you can play. In general, the more skills you learn, the better. For example, learning how to fence or ride a horse expands your repertoire. In some locations, it is possible to attend special high schools, such as the High School of Performing Arts in New York City, in which training for acting is an integral part of the curriculum. Being accepted to such a school usually requires doing an audition.

The best way to polish your acting skills is to practice. There are lots of opportunities to do so. Act in videos you and your friends make. Internet sites such as YouTube have made it possible for anyone to create and upload his or her work. In college, you will have the opportunity to work on student-made films as well as act in stage plays. This type of experience will give you a feel for what it is like to act on a film or television show. It will also give you the opportunity to experience working with a director and crew members. Don't restrict yourself to video. Participate in school plays. Many famous actors started out acting in plays in high school. See if your town has a community or summer theater that puts on plays and audition for a part in community theater productions. Many regional theaters (professional theaters that operate in cities other than New York) and summer theaters also offer acting classes. In the summer, check out sources such as *Variety* and backstage.com to locate films or television shows shooting in your area, and apply for a job as an extra. Doing an internet search on "background actors needed [city]" will bring up casting agencies in that city that are looking for background actors for productions. Practicing acting teaches you not only how to apply your skills but also how to recognize the areas where you lack expertise and need more work.

Internships

Internships are unpaid positions that allow a student to learn on the job. Students can start to apply for part-time or summer internships while in high school and participate in them during college. An internship gives someone a chance to work with experienced directors and actors and to observe how professionals approach the job. Internships can help students decide if acting is the right career for them. Some professional

A student intern takes notes and carries out errands for the director of a film.

community and regional theaters are required to hire actors who are members of the stage actors' union, Actors' Equity. However, many operate under an arrangement with Actors' Equity that allows them to hire a certain number of nonunion students for training purposes, and some offer internships. Acting interns perform small roles in stage productions at regional theaters. Check with the local theaters in your area to see what opportunities are available.

The film and television actors' union, SAG-AFTRA, offers internships to college students through its SAG-AFTRA Foundation. The SAG-AFTRA Foundation internships are designed to provide college students with the opportunity to learn about the film and television industry, including "communications, development, special projects, program management and general office administration." Students do not act in the productions, but they do learn how films and TV shows are made. It's important for interns to get contact information from everyone they work with. Such contacts could come in handy when looking for a job or job reference.

Being an intern gives a person a chance to make a good impression on industry professionals. It's important for interns to conduct themselves as professionals. Both when they are interning and when they are starting out in the professional world, attitude will be important. Interns and new actors need to show up on time and have a positive attitude. They must be polite to established actors, the director, and other professionals. Arrogance isn't appreciated even in established actors; it has no place in an actor who is starting out. Their job is to learn their craft—even those who graduate from well-known drama and film schools have much to learn. For background work and small parts, directors often hire the same actors over and over because they know they can count on them. Those who become successful are those who do their best work, no matter how small their part. People are more likely to get noticed and spark interest in a director if they are doing a great job in a small part than if they are doing mediocre work.

An acting student reads a part in class while her classmates take notes to critique her performance.

CHAPTER FOUR

Challenges and Pitfalls

Acting is a challenging profession, and a wide range of problems and issues can arise during the production of a film or TV show. Some problems can be foreseen. Others arise unexpectedly. Some challenges are technical. Others are personal. Every project presents unique challenges, but there are some pitfalls that actors commonly face.

Starting Out

The first problem an actor faces is getting work. There is a great deal of competition for acting roles. Even well-known actors don't work continuously— but they are paid large sums of money, so they don't need to worry about income between projects. Actors who are just starting out must build up their careers to the point where they can make a living as a background actor, supporting character actor, or voice actor; find a job that offers steady employment, such as a role in a daytime drama or TV series, or as an iconic character in a company's commercials; or become sufficiently successful to command a high salary. To achieve any of these goals, an actor needs determination and persistence.

To further complicate matters, to work in film or television, an actor must be a member of the film and television actors' union, SAG-AFTRA. To get a union card, one must be hired on a film, television show, or commercial. Since there are plenty of actors who are already members of the union, a nonunion actor has to be very impressive or unique to be hired and become eligible to join the union. Some actors choose to do stage work when starting out, in addition to trying to get hired for films or TV. There is more opportunity to do this in New York City, where many of the TV networks are headquartered, than in Los Angeles, the home of the major film studios, because of the Broadway and off-Broadway theater scene. New York is also the location where producers of Broadway plays recruit actors for touring companies, which perform Broadway plays in other cities around the United States. Applying for both stage and television/film jobs doubles an actor's chance of finding work. Being hired for a stage play both provides an actor with a professional credit and allows film and television agents, producers, and directors to see his or her work. Many film and TV actors started on the stage. One example is Kristin Chenoweth, who starred in Broadway shows such as *Wicked* before moving on to a career on several TV shows and as a singer. If other actors in a stage play also work in film or television, they could be valuable future contacts for an actor looking for film or TV work.

Another way to get a union card is to be hired as a background actor in a film or television show. This may be easier for those who live in cities other than New York and Los Angeles. Often films are shot "on location." If an actor lives in a city where a film is being shot, auditioning for a position as a background actor might result in a job, especially if a large number of background actors are needed. Because there are not as many actors looking for work in film and television away from the major production hubs, one's chances of being hired are greater. Once hired, the actor can apply for a union card.

Often young actors need to work at a nonacting job to support themselves. Because they need to have flexible hours that allow them to attend auditions, many choose to become temporary clerical workers, wait staff, or freelancers in a variety of jobs. They might do handyman work or fix computers on their own schedule. If you are considering a career as an actor, you might wish to take courses that teach you practical skills, such as those necessary for secretarial or computer services work, so that you can obtain a job with flexibility.

Actors have to be their own promoters. Even after they are hired for a production, they still need to continuously search for the next project. They need to make a constant effort to develop industry contacts and give directors, producers, and agents a chance to see their work. This usually means doing any workshop productions, staged readings of plays, and independent videos available, and taking any other opportunity that presents itself. It pays for actors to keep a list or file of every project they worked on, and the people they worked with, along with those people's contact information.

Actors need to keep an up-to-date curriculum vitae (CV). The CV is a form of résumé that documents the actor's education and the roles he or she has played in various projects. Actors should add any new projects to this document and also keep any good reviews. In addition, actors need a number of professional headshots (photographs of the actor's face). When applying for an audition slot, actors send the casting director the CV and a headshot.

Learning the Trade

No matter how effortless an actor makes a performance seem, the fact is that acting is a highly technical profession. One must learn to control one's body and speech and master a variety of other skills. The particular skills actors choose to learn depend on the type of roles they are interested in playing, as well as their personal talents. Some actors attend four-year colleges and even graduate school. Others attend acting schools or work with personal acting coaches. Even after they start getting jobs, many continue to take classes to expand the range of their skills. Not only does adding skills to one's repertoire make one eligible for a larger range of projects, but it gives one the chance to make more industry contacts. Even famous actors take lessons to learn to play a musical instrument, for example, or speak another language when a role requires it. The more proficient an actor becomes, the greater his or her chances of being hired.

Working on Location

One of the rigors that actors face is working on location—real places rather than a studio soundstage

Actors filming on location in the jungle face unpleasant conditions including heat, humidity, and insects.

or backlot. A soundstage is a building in which a film or TV show is shot. Portions of films are often shot in locations that would be hard to reproduce on a soundstage. Sometimes, filming takes place in the location where the film is set—for example, shooting a pirate movie in the actual Caribbean. Often, however, a location is chosen because its look is appropriate. For example, the *Lord of the Rings* trilogy was shot in New Zealand because its scenery provided a fantasy-like setting.

A Hollywood studio might not transport actors to Africa to film a picture set in the Sahara Desert. The exterior scenes could be shot in the Mojave Desert, which extends across southeastern California and western Nevada. That setting might not be much more pleasant for the actors, however. They would still have to work outside in the heat, sand, and wind. Location shoots tend to mean long days because of the expense of renting both the location and the equipment. The elements might play havoc with the actors' skin and hair, which would require constant touchups. If working in a foreign country, actors might be faced with language barriers when trying to communicate with the local population and crew, as well as limited choices of food or accommodation. They might have to contend with members of the press, photographers, and curious local people. Television shows are less likely than film productions to shoot in distant locations because they have smaller budgets. However, some shows, especially miniseries and made-for-TV movies, may require actors to shoot on location if, for example, it's too expensive to create an estate with a mansion and extensive grounds—as was the case with

Downton Abbey, which was shot at Highclere Castle in Hampshire, England. A scene might also be shot on location if special circumstances require it, such as a scene involving an explosion that had to be filmed on a bomb range for safety reasons.

It's not unusual for weather to cause problems when a film crew is working on location. Renowned director Francis Ford Coppola's filming of the Vietnam War film *Apocalypse Now* was shot on location in the Philippines. He transported a large cast and crew there for what was supposed to be five months of filming. The shoot turned into a fifteen-month ordeal due to delays caused by the country's stormy weather. A typhoon destroyed sets and locations, resulting in a two-month shutdown of filming while new locations were found and sets rebuilt. Some members of the cast and crew were kept on location, whereas others were transported back to the United States for weeks and then brought back. The rigors of making the film were captured in a documentary called *Hearts of Darkness*.

Criticism

Actors need to be able to take criticism. Once a film or television show is completed, anyone and everyone can see it, and everyone will have an opportunity to comment on it—from professional film and TV critics to local bloggers. If an actor becomes well known, he or she is subject to even more scrutiny. Reporters, photographers, and fans are all inclined to capture any information they can about the actor, and to comment on it. Some people's comments will be positive, but others will have negative opinions. Some will critique the actor's performance negatively for reasons that are beyond his or her control, such as badly written dialogue, dull directing, and poor camera work. Thus, actors may be blamed for a poor-quality film or TV show when the fault lies elsewhere, but at other times, critics will point out elements that the actor can work to improve.

Actors must learn to accept criticism as part of their job, evaluating it to find valid points, and letting the rest go. The same is true of positive comments. It's pleasant to receive praise, but it's important for an actor not to let praise go to his or her head. If actors become arrogant, they are less likely to take direction and adopt suggestions that would improve their performance. If they become hard to work with, they won't receive offers of work. It's far better for them to take both praise and criticism in stride.

Public Scrutiny

All actors who become recognizable to the general public through their appearances on TV or in films have particular problems they must deal with, not just the big stars. One issue they face is that, no matter where they are, they must be careful about what they say and how they say it, as well as what they do. At one time, actors only had to worry about the press following them and taking down what they said. Now that everyone has a cell phone with a video camera built in, anyone anywhere can record them and post information on the internet for everyone to see. It can be stressful to watch every word to make sure that nothing one says can be misconstrued as offensive.

The fact that they can be photographed at any time means that recognizable actors must always be careful about how they look and behave.

Even if actors are very careful and avoid making politically charged or discriminatory statements, the things they say can be quoted out of context, creating a negative impression. Even worse, sometimes rumors are started about actors, including about their personal lives, which can be irritating and frustrating, since it is virtually impossible to correct misinformation once it is spread. Every aspect of an actor's life is subject to public scrutiny, from where and what they eat to whom they are seen with. Often, every person they talk to is painted either as someone they're involved with or someone they're feuding with. In addition, both professional and amateur photographers love to catch them in unguarded moments when they are going about the activities of daily life.

Acting's Effect on Relationships

Being an actor can be hard on relationships with friends, significant others, and spouses. When actors are starting out, their schedules are unpredictable. They may be busy rehearsing and in production all day for several weeks, then have several weeks with no work. They will be running to auditions whenever they hear of one, and if they are chosen for a callback, they have to go back the next day, regardless of what they were planning to do. If chosen for a role, they might have to start immediately with preshoot preparations such as costume fittings, rehearsals, and shooting. Thus, if actors are lucky enough to get a role, they might have to cancel plans made with family and friends. This means they have to be sure to give their family members adequate attention when they are available, and the people in their life need to be willing to adjust to the unpredictable demands of the actor's life.

Granted, acting is not the only profession that is hard on relationships. The spouses of police officers and doctors face much the same issues. If actors become successful, they must deal with additional stressors that can affect their relationships because the press and public scrutinize every aspect of their lives, including their friends and families, if they can. Rumors, even if untrue, can add stress to a relationship. Relationships can remain sound, but people in this situation have to work at it.

Sexual Harassment

Many actors have reported experiencing sexual harassment or inappropriate sexual behavior from other actors, directors, and producers. Women are most often the targets of this activity, although there have been incidents that involved young men as well. Often the victims are young actors who have not yet made a name for themselves and therefore are vulnerable to being fired if a star, director, or producer is displeased with them. Television networks and Hollywood studios, and the companies they hire, have policies and procedures that actors can use to address sexual harassment.

Actors should be sure they know how to handle sexual harassment and inappropriate behavior if they encounter it. Time's Up is an organization that combats both sexual harassment and inequality for women in the entertainment industry. Their website provides information on how to handle sexual harassment. The organization has also set up the Time's Up Legal Defense Fund to help women with legal cases related to sexual harassment. It helps women in the entertainment industry and in other professions as well.

Acting Mishaps

Acting is not an occupation one thinks of as being perilous—except in the sense of not finding enough work to pay for food and rent. However, acting can sometimes be dangerous, especially when stunts are involved, as in superhero or action adventure films and TV shows. In the early days of films, there were no guidelines for protecting actors' safety during filming, and there were numerous incidents of actors being injured on set. For example, during the shooting of the famous chariot race in 1925's *Ben-Hur*, a stuntman and several horses were killed. *The Great Flood*, a 1928 film about Noah's Ark, featured a far-too-realistic scene of the population being swept away. As hundreds of thousands of gallons of water poured through the scene, three extras were killed and dozens more wounded. Eventually, the number of filming accidents led studios to create safety protocols for stunt performers. While modern safety rules and extensive rehearsals have cut down on the number of such incidents, it is impossible to eliminate accidents, which can be caused by weather, unexpected problems, or mistakes such as a miscalculation in jumping.

In addition, movie stunts have become larger and more impressive, involving many actors, vehicles, equipment, and pyrotechnics (explosions and fire). While professional stuntpeople perform many of the more complex stunts, actors are still often shot in scenes involving pyrotechnics, such as explosions, and they must run and jump over obstacles, and sometimes fight with weapons. Accidents involving both stuntpeople and actors still occur.

One of the most famous Hollywood disasters occurred during the filming of the "Time Out" segment of *Twilight Zone: The Movie* in 1983. In one sequence, the character played by actor Vic Morrow travels back in time to rescue two children from a US Army helicopter attack on a village during the Vietnam War. A stunt helicopter was flying low through pyrotechnic explosions that created smoke and flying debris. An explosion went off too close to the helicopter and damaged the tail rotor, which sent the helicopter out of control, and it crashed, killing Morrow and the two child actors.

Being an action hero is particularly hard on the body. During the filming of *Rocky IV*, actor Dolph Lundgren punched Sylvester Stallone so hard that it caused his pericardium (the sac around the heart) to swell, sending Stallone to the hospital for nine days. This wasn't Stallone's only injury. In the movie *First Blood*, one of his stunts was to tumble from a mountain ledge into a tree. The plot called for him to be hurt on the way down, and he certainly was. He broke several ribs hitting a branch along the way and let out a very realistic scream of pain. In *Armour of God*, martial artist Jackie Chan, who always does his own stunts, was supposed to jump from a castle wall to a tree. He missed the tree and fell 25 feet (7.6 meters), hit his head on a rock, and fractured his skull, requiring serious medical treatment. While filming the science-fiction film *Aeon Flux*, actress Charlize Theron landed incorrectly when performing a backflip and injured a disc in her neck—which could have paralyzed her, but she was lucky enough to recover. When making *Gothika*, Halle Berry struggled so hard with Robert Downey Jr. in one scene that she snapped a bone in her forearm and had to take three weeks off. While making *Thor: The Dark World* in 2013, Jaimie

SERENDIPITOUS ACCIDENTS

Not all accidents are life threatening, and sometimes an actor's mishap results in unexpectedly dramatic, or serendipitous, scenes. In *The Tomb of Ligeia*, characters played by actors Vincent Price and Elizabeth Shepherd are caught in a room in a mansion that is supposedly burning down around them. The scene turned out to be more authentic than expected when a carelessly lit cigarette accidentally ignited the set, which started to burn for real. According to Price's autobiography, director Roger Corman ordered the filming to continue—capturing a very realistic fire—and the very real horror of Price, who had a lifelong fear of being burned in a fire. (The actors were actually unharmed.)

Viggo Mortensen's performance in *The Lord of the Rings: The Two Towers* was enhanced by unplanned incidents.

Likewise, in *The Lord of the Rings: The Two Towers*, Viggo Mortensen, who portrays Aragorn, played a scene in which, believing two hobbits are dead, he kicks a helmet out of the way and breaks down in anguish. He did a great job of kicking the helmet and letting out a scream of grief before falling to his knees. It wasn't great acting though—Mortensen had kicked the helmet so hard he broke two toes.

In another scene, the audience sees Aragorn swing his sword to knock away a knife flying toward his face—a great stunt, only it was more like great reflexes, because the knife wasn't supposed to be in that location. It was misthrown.

Alexander, who plays the Asgardian Sif in the *Thor* movies, fell from a height, dislocated her shoulder, and chipped eleven vertebrae (bones in the spine).

Even nonexotic parts of the set can be dangerous. In 2015, during the filming of *Star Wars: The Force Awakens*, Harrison Ford's ankle was trapped by one of the hydraulic doors and broken.

TV shows are not without their dangers either. In an episode of *Law and Order: Special Victims Unit*, actress Mariska Hargitay suffered a collapsed lung when she landed wrong during the filming of an action scene.

On the lighter side, there are many blooper reels of TV outtakes, showing flubbed lines and wardrobe mishaps—or simply pieces of the set letting go or falling over. One thing is for certain: actors need to keep themselves in good physical shape to withstand the demands of on-set activity. And it wouldn't hurt to learn some stunt techniques, such as how to fall safely, even if one doesn't plan to become a stuntperson.

Coping with Challenges

Aspiring actors will encounter many challenges. Anyone serious about pursuing an acting career will most likely have to move to a large city, such as New York or Los Angeles, to find reliable work. For people who come from small towns, this can require considerable adjustment. Also, the cost of living in large cities is often so high that actors at the start of their career must share an apartment in order to afford the rent.

Director Woody Allen speaks with actress Selena Gomez during filming. Conflict can occur when a scene isn't coming together.

Actors have to work for long hours—from early morning makeup and costuming to shoots that last into the evening. They may have to spend hours in makeup and wear uncomfortable prostheses and heavy costumes. Some directors require a large number of shots of every scene. Others are testy when the actor is not giving exactly the performance they want. It is inevitable that, no matter how perfectly the production is planned and scheduled, there will be problems. Special effects and stunts won't always work as expected, equipment can malfunction, and the weather may refuse to cooperate on location.

When things go awry, the director, actors, and crew can all get irritated and frustrated. Delays cost money, and even directors are answerable to the producers and the studio in the event of cost overruns. When the director is irritable or worried, he or she may snap at the actors. But when actors are exasperated at the number of takes of a scene or the attitude of the director, they often can't vent their frustration at him or her because doing so could affect their ability to get projects in the future. Actors have to be careful to control their temper even when tired and upset. Starring actors in particular can set the tone for the rest of the cast.

If you are interested in becoming an actor and you work on small-scale projects such as YouTube videos or student film projects, you will likely learn firsthand how things go wrong. You may not be working on a professional project, but that is no excuse to lose your temper and behave badly. When you are learning the trade, that is the time to develop coping skills that will serve you well when you are in the professional arena, where the stakes are much higher. Actors need to learn how to handle themselves as well as manage other people when problems occur.

Actors are not the only people working long hours; the production crew is equally burdened. Actors need to be careful not to take their frustration out on crew members. The most important thing actors need to learn is how to remain calm when things go wrong. They have to be able to step back, realize that others are also under pressure, and not take things personally. This is not always easy to do, but it is a valuable skill. Often, allowing others who are upset to vent is enough to defuse a tense situation. Staying in control and being supportive of others will earn their appreciation and gain an actor a reputation as someone not easily flustered, with an aura of dependability—someone others want to work with. The reverse is also true: Actors who respond to provocation by snapping or yelling, or who harangue others for causing problems, will gain a reputation for being hard to work with—regardless of who provoked whom. Since it's virtually impossible to keep anything from being reported on the internet, it's likely that any conflict with an actor will become common knowledge. This can make it harder to get work in the future. Directors don't like to work with actors they believe are "difficult."

Therefore, no matter how long they have been on set in uncomfortable makeup or costumes, no matter how unreasonable the director seems to be in his or her demands, or however much actors feel that someone else is messing up, they must avoid being nasty to others involved in the production. The bad feelings this creates will only make it harder to work with others throughout the rest of the project. In addition, in TV and film, actors often depend on being recommended for work by other actors, directors, and producers. In some cases, actors have been recommended by makeup or costume designers who have worked with them. Treating everyone well can pay dividends in the future.

Actors have had long, successful careers in supporting roles playing particular types of characters. Here, actor Hugo Weaving *(left)* plays a henchman in *The Matrix*.

CHAPTER FIVE

From Acting to the Real World

Some film and television actors continue to act for their entire career. Even those who don't become stars will sometimes find steady employment as supporting, background, or voice actors. Actors with a distinctive look find steady work playing a certain "type," such as a henchman to the villain. Successful actors sometimes move from acting to directing or producing films or TV shows. Some even start their own production companies. Many actors who do not find regular work choose to pursue other careers, as do some successful actors who become tired of the physical and mental demands of the profession.

Directing and Producing

Some actors who become successful move from acting to directing. Some want to be more involved in the creative side of making movies or TV shows, or want to bring certain types of films to the screen, such as those that highlight social issues. These actors-turned-directors can provide useful insight into what makes people successful, not just actors or directors, but people in general. Rob Reiner, who played Archie Bunker's son-in-law in the sitcom *All in the Family* in the 1970s, has directed a number of hit movies. In the 1990s and 2010s, directing gave him a chance to examine social and political issues with films such as *Ghosts of Mississippi* and *LBJ.* In a *MovieMaker* interview, Reiner gives some advice for those interested in directing, which applies equally well to those who want to excel as actors—or for that matter, to life in general:

> *If you want to be a filmmaker ... go study humanities, or English, or art history, because whatever frames of reference you have, they're going to come into play when you start making movies. The technical part of making movies, you can learn that. But what you can't learn is different frames of reference.*

Ron Howard started his career as a child actor, playing Opie on *The Andy Griffith Show* and then, in his youth, Richie Cunningham on *Happy Days,* before graduating to the role of director. He has made such successful films as *Apollo 13, A Beautiful Mind, Cinderella Man, The Da Vinci Code,* and the 2018 *Star Wars* prequel *Solo.* In the case of *Solo,* Howard was brought in to take over the project after the original pair of directors was dismissed. The producers felt their vision for the film wasn't what they were looking for. In an interview in *Entertainment,* Howard said of taking over the project, "Sometimes people break up, and it's really sad, and it's really disappointing, but it

Director Ron Howard spent his childhood and youth as an actor. He's used these skills to become an accomplished filmmaker.

happens and we learned a lot from our collaborators and we're better filmmakers for it."

Another job on the other side of the camera is that of producer. Some actors who have become big stars or been successful on long-running TV series are given the title of "producer." In some cases, this is merely a way to give actors more money, since they get additional pay for this position. In other cases, however, the actors contribute to the producing side of the show as well as acting.

Timothy Olyphant, who played Raylan Givens on the TV series *Justified*, is one such actor/producer. He notes that for an actor on a series who is named a producer, the job is what one makes it. Olyphant wanted to be involved in the creative side of the series to the greatest degree possible, and he has worked with the other producing staff, writers, other actors, and set designers. He says he has taken advantage of the opportunity that goes with the title producer: "that's where all the fun is—in the kitchen."

Michael C. Hall, the star of the TV series *Dexter*, was already deeply involved in the creative process behind the show before he was made a producer in the third season of the series. In his case, the title was acknowledgment of the contributions he made to crafting the direction of the story, which revolved around his character. Hall used his position as producer to act as a conduit between the cast and producers when they had a concern about elements of the show. Hall also had a chance to direct in the third season. In an interview, he stated, "It's nice to be in a position where you're required to give people definitive answers so that they can all do their jobs. I felt much more required to be available to people in ways that I'm not when I'm just acting."

Some actors even start their own production companies, which allows them to develop projects they have a particular interest in. Actor Bryan Cranston, who played Walter White on the popular television series *Breaking Bad*, also acted as a producer starting with the third season. He liked the position so much he made producing his primary profession. He started a production company, Moon Shot Productions, which produced the 2018 series *The Dangerous Book for Boys*, for Amazon. Cranston says he wants "to be the overall guide to the big ship and how it's moving … It's a perfect time for me to step away from being up front and now take on a supportive role in television and really continue to look for those gems and really compelling stories to tell. And I'm excited about it."

Increasingly, actresses are becoming frustrated by the lack of opportunities for women to work behind the camera in Hollywood. Some are starting their own companies to make films. Reese Witherspoon and Bruna Papandrea both had this idea, and in 2012, they merged their independent companies to form Pacific Standard, which produced the film *Gone Girl* and the HBO television series *Big Little Lies*. Witherspoon took over sole control of the company in 2016 and subsequently joined with another company, Otter Media. The new joint venture is called Hello Sunshine and is dedicated to stories focused on women for film, TV, and digital platforms.

Margot Robbie, who was nominated for the 2018 Best Actress Oscar for the film *I, Tonya*, was also a producer on the film. Projects undertaken by her production company, LuckyChap Entertainment, include a TV series called *Shattered Glass* and a comedy for Hulu called *Dollface*. Robbie stated in an interview in the *Hollywood Reporter* that she's reached the point where she wants to make sure that when she finds a script she loves, it goes in the direction she feels it should.

Margot Robbie is one of several successful actresses who started their own production companies.

Moving On

Being an actor can make it difficult to learn the skills required for jobs in other fields. The fact is that individuals who want to pursue a career in acting are pretty much restricted to jobs that give them the flexibility to go to auditions and take time off when they win a role. This limits their options to jobs like waiting tables, temporary office work, and self-employment at freelance occupations. Therefore, it is advisable to decide sooner rather than later to pursue other options, such as enrolling in college or obtaining training in another field. Many child actors choose to leave the field when they grow up, pursuing other careers.

If you are thinking of pursuing acting as a profession, it can be useful to take secretarial or computer courses that give you skills to work at jobs that are temporary or those that provide flexibility. Actors who choose to pursue a mainstream career can apply for jobs as background actors when films or TV shows are being shot in their area, working at acting part-time. These people are not dependent on their acting income to pay their bills, so they can have an occasional job on the side. Although being an actor may not give one the technical skills required in other fields, the experience of pursuing a career in acting, and/or training to be an actor, can give one valuable experience that can lead to success in real-world careers.

Among successful actors who have left the industry for other careers are married stars Freddie Prinze Jr. and Sarah Michelle Gellar, who left acting for

LESSONS FROM ACTING

In a *Huffington Post* blog post from December 6, 2017, wellness expert Susan Shehata wrote that she started working as an actor at age nineteen. After ten years, she sought a profession that would better support her, and she became a wellness instructor. In her article, she describes several lessons she learned from acting. Here are a few. The first is that often factors other than an actor's talent or performance determine whether or not he or she is chosen for a project. Sometimes external factors, such as the desire to have a mix of different types of people in the cast, determine who is chosen. The same is often true in real life—a variety of factors not within one's control can determine whether or not a person is selected for a project. Therefore, the person must learn not to take setbacks personally, but put them behind them and keep working toward their goal. Second, a person must create his or her own opportunities. He or she is unlikely to find the perfect opportunity ready-made and waiting. In the real world, this might mean starting a business on the side while working, asking for a promotion at work, cultivating people who can help a person find a job in another industry, or learning a new skill that will allow someone to advance in their job or change to another. Third, listening to and acknowledging what others say, and supporting them wins people over. It can also lead to friendships and career opportunities. Fourth, a person must learn the difference between goals and expectations, and not commit to the latter so much that they miss other opportunities in life.

Goals are what a person is working to achieve. Expectations are a belief that a person will or should achieve something. If a person has the goal of getting a starring role in a movie or TV show, that is something he or she can work toward, learning the craft, attending auditions and making contacts, and earning ever larger parts. If people are convinced they will be failures in life if they don't become stars, then they are likely to miss the satisfaction of the accomplishments they make along the way. They might also end up miserable, even if they have what others would consider a satisfying life and career. In addition, it can make them reluctant to change direction because they haven't met their expectations, even if they find that they are not deriving the satisfaction they thought they would from their chosen career, and even if they encounter another type of opportunity they might enjoy more.

the food industry. Prinze became a chef and wrote a cookbook in 2016, *Back to the Kitchen*. In 2015, Gellar, star of *Buffy the Vampire Slayer*, started a company that produces organic baking mixes, called Foodstirs. For Gellar, being a celebrity has both an upside and a downside. On one hand, the fact that she is a star draws attention to her business endeavor. On the other, it makes it harder for her to be taken seriously as a businesswoman, which is important to her.

Many child actors leave the entertainment industry and seek other career paths as they grow up. For example, Charles Korsmo, who played Robin Williams's son in *Hook*, gave up acting as a teenager. After getting his degree in physics, he became an advisor to the Department of Homeland Security. He then graduated from Yale Law and became a professor. He says his experience as an actor helps him by making him less nervous when lecturing to large groups of students.

Michael Maronna, who starred as Big Pete on the TV show *Pete & Pete*, is an example of an actor who moved to a different position within the entertainment industry. He switched from acting to lighting, working as an electrician on shows such as *Shades of Blue*, *Elementary*, and *Nurse Jackie*, as well as the movie *Men in Black 3*, among other projects.

Some actors maintain more than one career at the same time. In *Avengers: Age of Ultron*, actor Jeremy Renner plays Hawkeye. The running gag in the movie about Hawkeye always renovating his house is an inside joke, because in real life Renner works in real estate as well as acting. Along with business partner

Kristoffer Winters, he buys high-end properties, renovates them, and resells them. He was already doing this at the time he was trying to get established as an actor. When his career got a boost from an Academy Award nomination for his role in *The Hurt Locker*, he was sleeping on the hardwood floor of a house he was restoring.

Real-World Benefits of Acting

Even if a person decides that acting is not the right career for them, studying acting can provide a number of benefits that can apply to any career. Acting teaches people confidence and poise. Confidence is the sense that a person can rely on himself or herself. People who are confident are willing to speak their minds

Acting experience can increase a person's poise and confidence when making business presentations.

and stand up for what they believe in. They are willing to put themselves forward for projects and to ask for promotions or raises when they think they deserve them. Confidence is not arrogance. Arrogance is the belief that a person knows best in all situations and is better than other people. Confidence is faith in oneself. Poise is the ability to remain calm and collected in high-pressure situations. Many people are self-conscious, and acting is one way to get over the fear of exposing one's feelings in front of other people. Acting in student films and videos is just as effective in building confidence and poise and getting over one's self-consciousness as working professionally as an actor.

Acting can help people stay physically fit. Actors' bodies are an important tool of the trade. Staying in shape is important, not only for appearance's sake, but also to have the stamina for a film or video project. The actions, and possibly stunts, required for a role can be physically demanding. Acting encourages people to exercise, which makes them heathier, allows them to move more gracefully, and increases their stamina. It is also a great way to reduce stress. Getting in the habit of exercising regularly can provide lifelong benefits.

Acting teaches a person to speak both clearly and effectively. It teaches him or her how to project emotion and use both voice and body language to convey a message. It also trains people to pick up on cues from other actors and makes them aware of how an audience is reacting to what they are saying, which allows them to adjust their presentation. Skills such as these are necessary for successful public speaking

Acting coach Lee Sherman gets her students moving at a filmmaking workshop in 2013.

engagements, sales, corporate presentations, teaching, law, and any other occupation where one needs to be convincing and persuasive.

Actors learn teamwork. Whether in workshops, rehearsals, or production, actors work as part of a team. For a project to be successful, they must work not only with other actors, but also with the production crew. Acting teaches a person how to collaborate with others. Actors learn to both contribute their ideas and compromise with others. They learn how to give and take constructive criticism to improve the project. They also learn to support other actors involved in the project, to create an environment in which the best production can be created. Actors learn to work with people with diverse ethnic backgrounds and appreciate others' feelings and cultural viewpoints.

In order to portray characters, actors learn to put themselves in other people's shoes, understanding and adopting viewpoints other than their own. This helps them comprehend the nature and concerns of other people, an ability that benefits people in both their personal and business relationships.

Being an actor takes hard work and persistence. Finding work requires constantly pursuing opportunities. Once they are hired, actors work hard—often from early in the morning until late in the evening. They sometimes work in environments that are uncomfortable. Therefore, if they work at other jobs, they are well prepared to meet tight schedules, endure difficult working conditions, and work outside of regular business hours.

Actors are used to developing their characters through independent research and practice. They know they are responsible for contributing their best work to make a project successful. This ability to work independently and deliver high-quality work on time is a desirable trait in business. Actors are creative. They take the basic qualities of a character and create a unique, believable person. They are skilled at inventing different approaches and applying different concepts. They can often view a situation or product from a unique perspective. Creativity can be a benefit in many other professional pursuits, from creating a product to producing a special event. It often pays off when trying to solve a problem or develop a new business strategy, and therefore can contribute significantly to a person's professional success.

Actors get used to working in an environment filled with people and equipment. They learn to keep their concentration and focus even when faced with interruptions, distractions, and requests for help from others. Actors learn time-management skills, handling personal demands and professional obligations at the same time. Actors have to juggle the demands of film or television shooting, publicity activities, and the demands of their family. They have to be aware of how they look and behave at all times. Thus, they have experience working under pressure. They understand how to schedule their time and find support. They learn to find time to take care of themselves, to keep themselves healthy, even when they are busy, so that they don't become overwhelmed and burn out. The entertainment industry isn't the only field where a job can take over a person's life. Therefore, learning to balance work and personal life can lead to significantly stronger and healthier relationships regardless of the person's profession.

Being an actor is a creative and fulfilling profession, but it is also mentally and physically demanding. One of the most satisfying aspects of being an actor is the chance to experience what it is like to be different people, and to convey the feelings and experiences of a character to people who view a film or TV show. When actors succeed in making audiences care about the characters they portray, they can gain respect and admiration. Thus, an acting career can provide a great deal of satisfaction, despite the hard work involved.

GLOSSARY

automated dialogue replacement (ADR) The process of substituting dialogue recorded in a studio for that on a soundtrack.

backlot An area of the studio complex that contains exterior scenery and buildings for use in shooting films and TV shows.

callback A followup audition when a film or TV show's stars are being decided.

catchphrase A phrase from a film or TV show that is commonly used in regular conversation.

choreographer The person who designs the dance sequences for a film or TV show.

close-up A shot of an actor's face.

curriculum vitae A detailed résumé that explains a person's professional history and qualifications.

flub To mess up.

freelance To work for someone on a project-by-project basis, not as a full-time employee.

gaffer A person in charge of lighting for film and TV.

harangue To use forceful words when speaking to someone.

location A place where filming or taping takes place other than the studio complex.

persistence Making a continuous effort.

phrasing The way in which a word is pronounced, such as clipped or drawn out.

preshoot Shots taken prior to the start of production to establish the proper lighting and to ensure that costumes and makeup look correct.

proficient Skilled.

property An original script, series concept, or a novel or work from another media.

prosthesis A shaped piece of plastic, latex, foam rubber, or other material glued to an actor's skin to change the look of his or her face.

reaction shot An extreme close-up of an actor's face that captures his or her response to what he or she hears or sees.

serendipitous A chance occurrence with a positive outcome.

shooting schedule A list of dates and times on which scenes in a movie or TV show will be shot.

soundstage A building at the studio where a TV show or film is shot.

soundtrack The audio portion of a film, including words, music, and sound effects.

stunt A complex feat, such as jumping from a high cliff or running through fire, done by professionals for film or TV.

visual effects (VFX) Special effects created on a computer system.

FOR MORE INFORMATION

Books

Callahan, Dan. *The Art of American Screen Acting, 1912–1960*. Jefferson, NC: McFarland & Company, 2018.

O'Neil, Brian. *Acting As a Business*. New York: Vintage Books, 2014.

Pudovkin, V. I. *Film Technique and Film Acting*. Seattle, WA: CreateSpace Independent Publishing Platform, 2015.

White, Daniel. *Acting for Film and Television*. Seattle, WA: CreateSpace Independent Publishing Platform, 2013.

Wong, Judy Go. *How to Start an Acting Career Right Where You Live*. Seattle, WA: CreateSpace Independent Publishing Platform, 2016.

Websites

Backstage
https://www.backstage.com
Website with a variety of articles on acting and a listing of casting calls and auditions.

SAG-AFTRA
https://www.sagaftra.org
The film and television union site, with information on its activities, including its internship program.

Variety
http://variety.com
The industry publication for the film and television industries.

Videos

Anatomy of a Great Actor
https://www.youtube.com/watch?v=Iz2Fa1d1fRc
On this video, successful actors discuss what makes an actor's performance effective on screen.

Viola Davis on Acting
https://www.youtube.com/watch?v=a-f4DDnGSBc
Actress Viola Davis explains how to approach acting to achieve a successful performance.

Online Articles

"Best Acting Websites." StageMilk. Accessed March 15, 2018. http://www.stagemilk.com/best-acting-websites.

Breman, Phil. "The Basic Rules of Acting: Things Every Actor Should Know." The Balance Careers. February 28, 2018. https://www.thebalance.com/acting-get-that-part-1283504.

Cannon, Dee, and Lyn Gardner. "Character Building: What Makes a Great Actor?" *Guardian*. May 9, 2009. https://www.theguardian.com/stage/2009/may/09/character-building-great-actor.

Jackson, Dan. "The Wildest Things Daniel Day-Lewis Has Done to Prepare for Roles." The Thrillist. January 19, 2018. https://www.thrillist.com/entertainment/nation/daniel-day-lewis-method-acting-stories.

Ohikurae, Judith. "How Actors Create Emotions: A Problematic Psychology." *Atlantic*. March 10, 2014. https://www.theatlantic.com/health/archive/2014/03/how-actors-create-emotions-a-problematic-psychology/284291.

INDEX

Page numbers in **boldface** are illustrations.

location, 13, 20, 27, 34–35, **35**, 41, 55–59, **57**, 69

looping, 43

makeup artist, 20, 22–23, 26–27, **26**, **33**, 34, 40, 69, 71

Netflix, 5–7

persistence, 14, 53, 86

phrasing, 45

post-career possibilities, 79, 82–83

postproduction, 29, 40

preproduction, 29, 33

preshoot, 34, 62

producer, 14, 17–19, 24, 27, 29–30, 54–55, 63, 69, 71, 74–77

proficient, 56

property, 33

prosthesis, **33**, 34

reaction shot, 37, **37**

Robbie, Margot, 77, **78**

Screen Actors Guild– American Federation of Television and Radio Artists (SAG-AFTRA), 6–7, 50, 54

screenwriter, 19

script, **12**, 13, **15**, 17, 19, 27, 29–30, **31**, 32, 41, 45, 77

serendipitous, 66

set, **4**, 10, **11**, 13–14, **16**, 18–20, 22–23, 27, 32–34, **35**, 37, 40, 58–59, 63–64, 66, 68, 71, 76

sexual harassment, 63

shooting schedule, 18, 26, 34

soundstage, 41, 56, 58

soundtrack, 40–41, 43

special effects, 18, 22, 27, **33**, 34, 40, 42, 69

streaming services, 6

Streep, Meryl, 38–39, **39**

student films, 70, 84

stunt, 10, 13, 22, **23**, 64–65, 67–69, 84

supporting actor, 7–8, 42, 53, **72**, 73

visual effects (VFX), 22, 40

voice actors, 9, 43, 47, 53, 73

voice-overs, 9, 41–43

YouTube, 7, 47, 70

ABOUT THE AUTHOR

Jeri Freedman has a bachelor's of arts degree from Harvard University. She is the past director of the Boston Playwrights' Lab, an organization that produced original plays in Boston, Massachusetts. Her play *Choices*, cowritten with Samuel Bernstein, was staged at the American Theatre of Actors in New York City. She is also the author of more than fifty young adult nonfiction books, including *Exploring Theater: Stage Management in the Theater*, *Exploring Theater: Directing in the Theater*, *Getting to Broadway: How* Annie *Made It to the Stage*, and *Getting to Broadway: How* Wicked *Made It to the Stage.*